The Silence of Awareness

Title: The Silence of Awareness. Poems
© Nanne Nyander 2025.
www.nannenyander.se
Publisher: BoD · Books on Demand, Östermalmstorg 1,
114 42 Stockholm, Sweden, bod@bod.se
Print: Libri Plureos GmbH, Friedensallee 273,
22763 Hamburg, Germany
Cover, book design and painting by Nanne Nyander.
ISBN: 978-91-8080-132-4

Today is a good day to wake up.

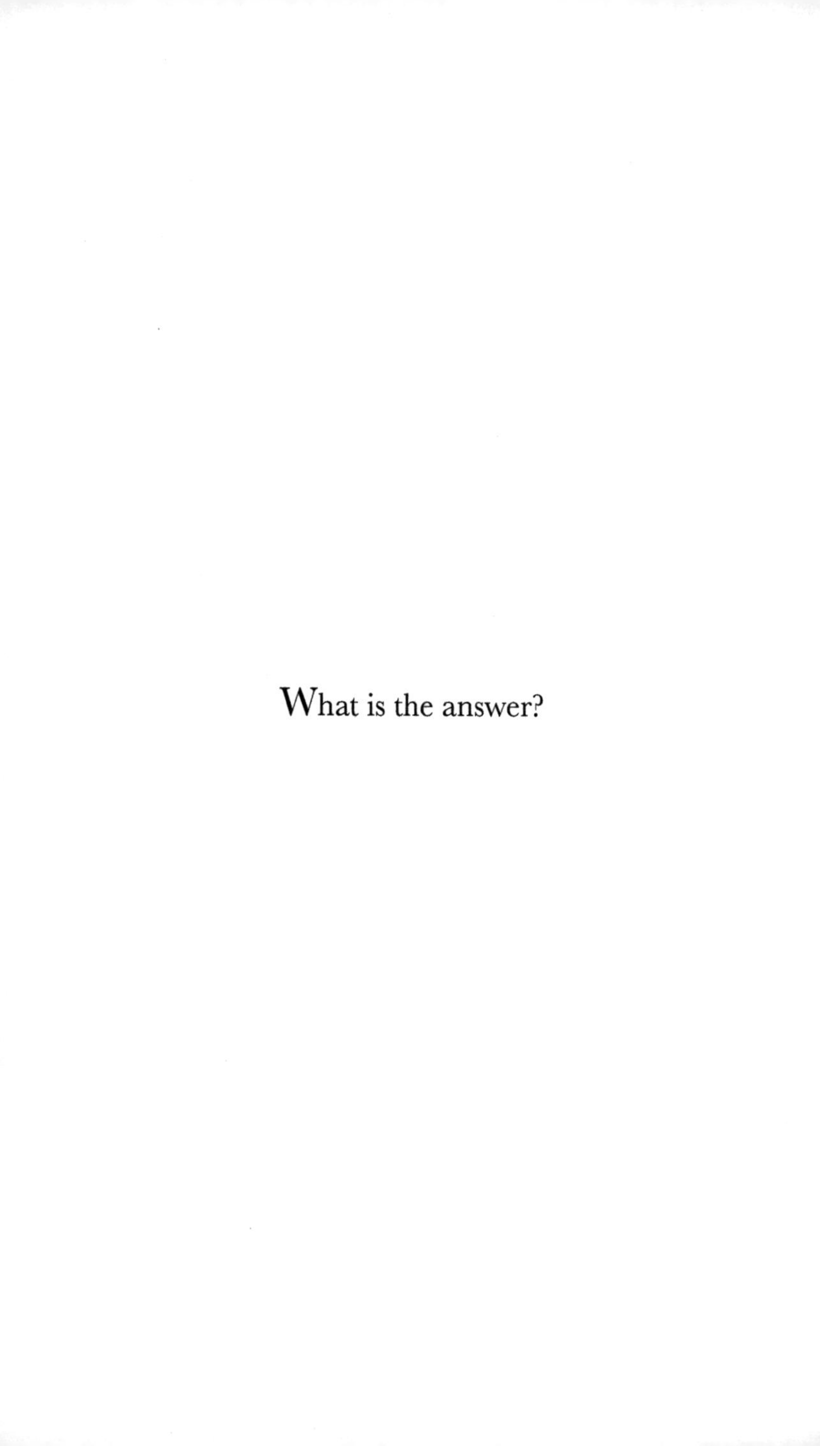

What is the answer?

1.

I'm here to experience,
I'm not here to be found.
I'm nothing, I'm everything,
I'm nowhere, I'm everywhere.
I have no borders,
so what is going to find what?

2.

Thoughts floating around in awareness.
Am I also a thought in awareness,
or,
am I awareness,
and the me I thought was I,
is just a thought?
How funny,
me thinking me was something.
Who would have thought,
the me being something not existing.
The me is a thought,
a very persistent thought,
but now it's vanishing.
I'm so much bigger than
I could ever have imagined.
I am nothing.
Nothing is everything,
everything is nothing.
That's what I am.
I am not a thought.
I'm reality itself.

3.

I enter the day with an open heart
and an empty mind.
I am awake.
Thoughts come and go.
Still,
I am awake.

4.

Does a fish feel lonely?
Does it know that it's part of a great ocean?
Does the ocean know
that it's a part of Mother Earth,
or does it feel apart from everything,
believing it's on its own,
moving around, separate from everything else?
Does Mother Earth think?
What would its thoughts look like?
I'm a tiny, lonely planet in this vast universe,
I'm lost, please help me to find me.
Or is it content with just being?
Is the universe separate from me?
From out there I'm nothing,
I'm not even visible,
just a speck of dust that no one sees.
I am no one.
I can see you.
To me, you are special,
to me, you are not just a speck of dust,
to me, you are everything,
to me, you are me.

5.

I'm empty.
I'm free.
I do not worry.
I do not think.
I stay at home and I don't accept invitations
into the mind,
into the mind and its endless labyrinth of thoughts.
If I do accept the invitation,
it's like quicksand,
like entering the land of forgetfulness,
no longer remembering who I am.
Pointless thoughts,
moving around in space.
I leave them be,
and just stay quiet inside,
and just be.

6.

To focus is a challenge,
do I have to focus?
Things just happen.
It feels like I need a jumpstart sometimes,
and from there, things just happen.
Has it always been like that,
and the mind claims the doing and deciding,
as *its* doing?
No need to plan,
but planning might happen.
I can't decide,
but deciding is happening.
I don't have the motivation to do,
but doing is still happening.
Am I a happening?

7.

Am I dissolving into nothing?

8.

I'm empty and full at the same time,
depending on which way I lean.
I lean this way and
I'm in the tumultuous land of thought,
I lean back and I'm in heavenly quietness
that soothes my whole being.
I'm so much more than I *think* I am.
I'm everything.
I'm nothing.

9.

The feeling of emptiness is filling me with love,
love for everything.
The feeling of nothingness, embraces my being,
like being embraced by the universe,
and embracing the universe at the same time.
We are one, and one is all.
All is love in disguise.

10.

If I leave everything alone,
will I wake up?
I need to leave that one alone too,
the one who's leaving everything alone,
the one who thinks she's going to wake up.
How to do that?
It's all thought, that one does not even exist,
she's just a thought.
A very persistent thought.
A thought that has wrapped itself around me,
suffocating me.
But it's all a thought.
I'm here,
nothing is suffocating anything.
The storyteller is seen through,
it's an imposter,
making me believe it's me.
Me does not exist.
It's a fascinating story,
hard to let go of,
but it's still a story,
and so is the one trying to let go.
I can see it, I can feel it.
Why is this not enough?
Why is the illusion still so persistent?
Will I ever wake up?
And, yes,
that one is a thought too.

11.

Sleep no more.
I'm vigilant of thoughts coming to drag me away,
drag me away,
far, far away to the land of oblivion.
I'm standing firm and solid in reality.
The mind invites me to tag along
to the most intriguing places.
But I'm on my guard,
I'm not as gullible as I once was.
No more sleepwalking in the land of Oblivion.
I'm the truth,
I'm reality,
I am Awake.

12.

Emotions, sensations, thoughts,
nothing belongs to me,
nothing is mine, everything is me.

13.

Heaven is near, fear no more,
heaven is here, be no more,
lost in thoughts about a better world.
A better world than what's lurking
in the mind of the seeker.
Heaven is always here,
inside and outside as this nothingness we all belong to,
we all is.
Nothing is heaven and heaven is nothing
and everything.
Hell is the entrapment of mind,
entangled in thoughts about a better world,
thoughts about heaven.
Heaven is here.
I'm here,
and so are you,
my beloved angel.

14.

If I was a snail,
would you look at me and say
that I'm beautiful?
If I lose myself,
would you find me,
or would you let me be lost?
If I was you,
would you hug me
and hold me tight,
till we accept that we are one?
If I was still here,
would I lose you?

15.

The past is not just a long time ago,
it's also one second ago.
But the past does not exist,
time does not exist.
So what's the difference?

16.

Back to the beginning.
This is the same world,
same but different.
Is it more quiet,
or is it I?
Is it the mind moving backwards into itself,
lacking things to entice the me with?
Me does no longer respond,
me does not exist.
It's quiet,
but full of sounds at the same time.
How can it be?
The mind does not mind anymore.
Did the mind wave the white flag,
or was it I?
No end,
no beginning.
Just quiet.

17.

The end is near,
and I'm still here.
Why did I walk astray,
trying to find myself out there,
when I've been here the whole time?
The end is near.
The end is here.

18.

Looking at thoughts.
Am I still an I,
looking for I?
Who's the one looking?
I can see thoughts,
I can sense a me,
or a centre.
Is the centre I'm aware of I?
What's aware of the centre?
I feel like a whirlpool,
where nothing can exist.
What *am I?*
Everything disappears into nothing,
am I still here?
I'm not solid anymore,
never was,
except seemingly in thought.
Thoughts moving around like crazy,
but they are at a distance,
I can't grab hold of them,
they are only sensed.
Am I a black hole,
sucking in everything,
The Big Bang in reverse?

19.

Mind is racing more than ever,
but I have no idea what it's saying.
Its noise is overwhelming,
I can't think,
I can't focus.
Is it supposed to be like this?
What if it never stops?

20.

Invisible me, no thoughts to see,
no thoughts.
Invisible me, running past a tree,
running for the sea.
Listen,
I'm the sound of rain,
pouring over me.
Invisible me,
nothing to see,
nothing to be,
nothing.

21.

Save me from me,
save me from the thought of me.
Me does not exist,
it's all just thoughts.
Me is empty,
no thoughts no self.
I no longer have a body,
I no longer have a past or future.
Me is empty,
empty of worries floating around
as thoughts in space,
thoughts that I used to take for a me.
Me is empty,
and the emptiness is full.
I'm nothing and everything at the same time.
Save nothing.
Nothing doesn't need saving.
Nothing is already all there is.

22.

The commentator is getting very boring,
the commentator is getting bored.
No one is listening,
no one is taking the commentator seriously.
The commentator is just rambling.
It's not entertaining anymore.
It's just another sound in the universe
where nothing and everything
are going on at the same time,
no time.
Thoughts are appearing,
heart is beating,
stars are collapsing.
Am I in the middle of everything,
or is everything in the middle of me,
or am *I* everything?

23.

I'm living in the land in between,
where no thoughts can land.

24.

I'm always here,
but the mind tells me I'm going places,
I'm going on a long journey to find me.
Without the mind telling me stories,
I'm here,
without any doubt.
With the mind babbling along,
I'm here,
but I struggle to believe it.
The mind tells me all sorts of things,
makes me believe I'm going to find me,
find me somewhere else,
another time,
another place.
I'm never here, it's never now,
the mind convincingly tells me.
I wonder why I still believe it?
What makes me keep the mind so close,
listen to every word it says,
as if it was the truth?
I can clearly see
it does not know what it's talking about.
It's just talking,
nonstop,

telling me anything to keep me occupied,
to keep me from exposing this imposter,
I've been calling me.
It keeps telling me lies,
but the I does not like lies,
and the mind does not enjoy the truth.
We are obviously not a good match.
It's time to break up,
time to expose this imposter.
Time to wake up.
I'm here,
I am truth,
I am.

25.

I'm rambling, can I still love myself?
I make mistakes, can I still love myself?
I am not perfect, can I still love myself?
I'm human, can I still love myself?

26.

Far, far away, in an empty castle,
a dragon has been slumbering quietly
for many long years.
Then suddenly something slowly woke it up.
Now it's consuming everything I have built up,
my sandcastle has turned into ruins.
It keeps destroying everything I thought was me.
Till I suddenly one day realise,
I am the dragon.

27.

Thoughts are moving around in awareness,
but why is it using my voice?
Is it to make me think it's me?
Is it really *my* voice,
or is it just that it's been there so long
that I got used to thinking it's me?

28.

Is this a feeling?
Is this a thought?
Am I here?
Everything is empty,
everything is silent.
Is that a thought?
Everything is nothing,
and *I* have no separate room in it.
There are feelings, there are thoughts,
but they don't belong to a me.
Everything is empty,
the emptiness is full of nothing and everything
simultaneously.
Nothing belongs to a me.
Everything *is* me,
and me is nothing.

29.

I move as the wind when nothing is moving,
I'm moving too fast,
on an express lane that does not exist.
I move as my life depends on it.
I move so fast that I'm standing still.
I'm moving,
not moving,
feeling dizzy,
a feeling of losing the ground under my feet,
losing track of time,
losing myself in the nothingness.
I move too fast,
and I don't move at all.
I'm losing everything,
nothing is left.
Can this be right?
Nothing is left,
I'm nothing and so is everything else,
nothing else.
Nothing can't move,
I'm nothing.
Still,
I'm moving too fast.

30.

See me for what I am.
I don't know what I am,
so how can *you* know what I am?
Does that mean that you can't see me?

31.

Someone is here,
but it's not me.
Can I call it a someone,
or is it more a something?
Something is here looking for itself.
Where do I fit in in all this?
How do I stop watching this charade?
Do I have to be in on this, or can I just leave it be?
Leave it to do its searching on its own.
I'd rather do nothing,
I'd rather just be.
It's neither someone,
nor something,
it does not exist,
it's just thoughts,
images,
sensations,
moving around in nothingness.
It's dangerously captivating,
and highly addictive.
But it has nothing to do with me,
me does not exist.

32.

Am I moving away from reality?

33.

I'm an octopus,
I use my tentacles to sense if everything is ok.
I ramble,
I use words to change the energy between us,
I use words to see if everything is fine.
Is it safe?
I think I can alter the sticky energy you send out,
by talking,
by saying words,
words that almost make sense.
I ramble,
I talk too fast.
Why?
I thought I was the quiet one.
Words I use to calm the energy around me,
so that I can be at peace.
I'm a bat,
I use sounds to navigate,
is everything ok?
How do you feel?
Are you angry?
Have I done something wrong?

Hardly anyone tells the truth,
so I don't ask,
because then I have to decipher what the words
coming out of your mouth really mean.
When my sounds bounce back,
I can feel if I have managed to smooth the energy,
smooth it so that I can be at peace,
so that I can be calm.
I feel what everyone is feeling.
I'm a wave in a big ocean.
When the wave close to me gets muddy,
I can feel it.
After all,
we are all the same ocean.

34.

Feelings of possible regrets are coming up,
stirring around in the feeling pot.
I thought I was ok,
now you're digging up meaningless memories,
memories that I was fine with,
never felt any doubt,
but now you're throwing it in my face,
and I become confused and start to doubt.
Did I really do the right thing?
How can a fleeting thought have so much power?
I don't give it attention,
but the invitation is there,
and I can feel it's lingering,
staying close by,
just in case I change my mind.
It's just a thought,
it's just a thought.
I thought I could handle thoughts.
But who am I, who thinks,
and feeds the thoughts?
I can still feel the pull of the doubting thought,
lingering in the background.

One meaningless thought,
can become a huge dragon.
I used to be the dragon slayer,
but there is no need to slay dragons no more.
They are just here to show me the way,
the way back to what I am.
I'm here,
and everywhere,
I'm everything,
I'm nothing,
I'm the dragon.

35.

What is still in the mind,
stirring up confusion?
Everything is so simple without thought
trying to make things complicated.
Everything is simply very simple.

36.

Being a human being is not an easy ride,
being a human is inhuman.
It's ok as a sidekick,
but I'm so much more than that.
I'm nothing.

37.

When the infinite blossoms within nothingness,
I'm here making the seemingly impossible, possible.
I'm here,
in the illusion of time and space.
I'm the grand mirage,
now you can see me,
now you can't.
I'm here,
but not here.

38.

Fear of feeling good,
fear that something bad will happen if I feel good.
Feeling miserable is my curse in life,
I have to feel miserable to prevent bad things
from happening.
The me is an intriguing character.
Does the me think it's God?

39.

If I don't exist,
what am I still doing here?

40.

This is it.
So simple,
so difficult.
This is all there is.
Me is an illusion,
me does not exist.
Still, me is sitting here drinking tea,
or is drinking tea just happening?
Me does not exist.
Sitting is happening,
writing is happening,
listening to music is happening.
Me does not exist.

41.

I'm here,
I feel, see, hear.
No need to analyse,
no need to commentate on everything.
Just be.
I'm here,
I feel, see, hear.
No thoughts about the past or future
is holding me imprisoned.
I'm here.
There is nothing more than here and now.
I'm here.
No sane person would ever leave this peace.
But we are all a little insane,
at war with everything.
Even when alone,
we battle a private war in our own heads.
Why would we ever want to exchange this peace
for that?
We are all so innocent,
innocently insane.
I'm here,
I feel, see, hear.
I'm here.

42.

Who is the one that wants to listen,
or doesn't want to listen, to thoughts?

43.

Thought is a fantasy landscape.
I have tried to navigate through this confusing terrain,
but it keeps changing,
because it's all in my head.
I always thought we should come into this world
with a map or a manual,
on how it all works.
But how can there be such a thing,
when everything keeps changing all the time,
it's not even real.
There are no maps that are useful
on this trip we call life,
no maps for this imaginary world.
In this world,
everything keeps changing,
and so does this character I thought was I.
But what *I am* is not changing.
I have been here the whole time,
untouched by the changes the mind presented to me.
They have always just been invitations into the illusion.
I used to accept the invitations all the time,
I thought it was mandatory,
now I know, it's not,
it's just an invitation.
I'm here,
I'm free.

44.

How hard can it be to accept that these thoughts,
seemingly in my head,
are not *my* thoughts.
When I'm in my quiet place,
I can see the thoughts appearing and disappearing,
but when the chaos of life shows up,
then *I am* my thoughts,
they take me over,
they possess me,
they drown me.
I manage to swim to the surface for brief moments,
but then I feel like I'm drowning all over again.
When will this stop?
I know,
that's just a thought too.

45.

Do I live here, or am I just visiting?

46.

My head is full of fog,
I can't think.
Thoughts are still here,
but the effort to follow them is diminishing.
The past is a blur,
the future is non-existent.
I'm trying to plan,
but thoughts won't cooperate.

47.

I'm moving around in empty space,
and so is everything else.
Sometimes I bump into a sound or a thought,
we connect and let go at the same time.
Sounds appearing and disappearing.
Self is appearing and disappearing.
Nothing is leaving any trace.
Thoughts are appearing and disappearing.
Nothing is leaving nothing behind.
Everything is fleeting,
like waves.
Everything is moving like waves,
appear, disappear,
appear, disappear.
And here I am,
appearing and disappearing.
But before everything,
I am.

48.

Come home!
I can hear it loud as thunder.
The search is over,
you're home,
be home,
stay,
just be.

49.

Rain is pouring over me,
beautiful rain, where have you been?
One single drop could have been everywhere,
everything.
It might even have been a part of this body.
If a drop of water could speak,
what would it say?

50.

Everything is leaving me.
I'm living on the outside, looking in.
I rearrange my life unconsciously,
for me to be on the outside.
On the outside is where I feel I belong.
Being on the outside is what I am familiar with.
I can't belong,
I can't be on the inside.
I don't belong,
I don't know how.
Not belonging is uncomfortably comfortable.
I do belong,
I belong on the outside.

51.

Emptiness is screaming loudly in a silent voice,
I'm here, stop looking,
no looking will lead to finding.
I'm still.
Still trying not to look for what I am.
You can't try *not to look.*
Do or do not, there is no try.
Finding is an illusion,
floating around as bait in a future that does not exist.
Luring me to carry on looking for the non-existing me.

52.

The mind is brilliant,
but now I'm better prepared.
I know its tricks, I know not to get on the train.
The train of thoughts can take me on an endless
journey,
mostly to places I don't find fascinating anymore.
I still sometimes find myself on the train,
but now I know where the emergency brake is.
I'd rather sit on a hill far, far away,
and just watch the trains passing by.

53.

She who thinks she knows, does not know.
She who knows that she does not know,
is on her way to liberation.

54.

What am I doing here?

55.

Whatʼs real?
Sensations are real,
there are sensations, arenʼt there?
Is feeling the sensations separate from the sensations,
or are there just words separating the two?
Without the words, are they one?
Are sounds and hearing the sounds the same?
Nothing is really separating the two.
But nothing canʼt separate,
nothing glues it all together,
nothing makes it all one.
Is it language thatʼs separating everything
into tiny pieces?
Are there any borders between anything?
The me can separate everything into smaller and
smaller pieces,
if the me moves in the other direction,
and pieces it all together again,
will the me suddenly disappear,
disappear into the whole,
into nothing?

56.

I am, is life.
Everything is seen.
A thought moves past me
like a butterfly in the wind.
Sensations are like melting snow,
they appear and can be felt strongly,
but slowly they melt into nothing,
nothing as water touching this body.
Comforting water washes over everything,
like pleasant sensations after a turmoil of
feelings I can't control.
But I don't exist,
no need to control anything,
everything just is.
I am, is everything.
I am, is life.
I am life.

57.

Can you see me cry,
cry for help,
when all you see is you?

58.

Feel to be free,
free from all the disturbance in the mind,
free from strange emotions,
emotions and thoughts that I cannot pinpoint.
They are moving around in space,
and that's fine,
if they just hadn't been exactly where I am.
Is this how it is,
to be one with everything?

59.

Thoughts are coming up,
but it is seen.
Not my thoughts,
the me doesn't own them,
the me is nowhere to be found,
it's just a sense of a me.
The sense of me claiming everything as mine,
my thoughts,
my sensations,
my problem,
my, my, mine.
An emotion is coming up,
the me says it's an uncomfortable emotion,
me connects it with an uncomfortable thought.
Stop!
An emotion is coming up, the emotion is seen,
a thought appears, it is seen.
With no me and mine,
everything is fine.

60.

This is it.
You call me by my true name.
I'm home.
Me is lost,
but I am home,
has always been.
Me is still searching,
but I am home.
Me is nowhere to be found,
how can it still be searching?

61.

In another world, another time,
what would normal look like?

62.

The me is heavy to carry around,
the me is like grabbing onto a heavy stone,
and carrying it around without noticing what I'm doing.
Why not just drop it?

63.

If I disappear,
will I still be able to write,
or is this even me writing?
I am a poem, not yet written.
Will I write it,
or is it out there to be found?
Found by whom?
The me has a ghostwriter.
Life seems to already be written,
like a poem appearing in front of me.
I'm not writing,
it is written,
I'm not living,
it is lived,
Life is lived,
but not by a me.
I am a poem,
not yet written.

64.

I'm totally alone in this universe.
I am the only subject,
everything else is an object.
I'm totally alone.

65.

I see you get hurt and the pain is unbearable.
I see your pain,
your pain is mine.
I feel your pain,
your pain is mine.
There are no borders,
I feel too much,
I feel everyone's pain,
everyone's emotions,
but my own.
Maybe adding my own emotions and pain
on top of this, would be too much.

66.

Nothing is happening,
a lot of nothing is happening,
a lot of nothing is happening simultaneously.
I get all confused,
but what am I, that can get confused?
Confusion is happening,
that's all there is.
Nothing is still happening.

67.

I used to remember how it was to be alive.

68.

I am nowhere to be found,
I'm spread all over the world.
I am nowhere and still everywhere.
I am the sound that's sounding.
I am the breath that is breathed.
I am the sensations sensed.
I am nowhere to be found,
still, I am everything,
and I'm everywhere.

69.

Can you feel a thought appearing,
or do you see it?
Can you hear it?
Can you hear a feeling,
or do you see it?
Can you sense the difference
between a thought and a feeling?
Is there a difference?

70.

Hope follows me wherever I go,
but Hope is my biggest obstacle.
She keeps me focused on the future,
focused on becoming.
Despair is holding my hand,
he keeps me stuck in the past.
Hope and Despair walk hand in hand with me,
happily distracting me from what I am,
distracting me from reality,
inviting me to look anywhere but here and now.
Hope acts as my friend,
Despair acts as my enemy.
Sometimes Despair feels more comforting than Hope,
but they are the same character with different clothing.
I'm here, I'm now,
I am reality and I have the power to turn down any
and all invitations into the land of illusion.
Hope is just a thought,
and so is Despair.
I alone is real.

71.

I cannot remove myself from your
world of illusion,
but I can remove you from mine,
by not thinking about you.
Isn't that amazing?

72.

There's nothing left to do,
than to just do whatever comes my way.
No motivation,
just follow the breadcrumbs,
and hope I get out of this entrapment.
I can't even see the light anymore.

73.

What's the difference between you and me?
You say you have woken up,
I say I have not.
What's the difference between
awake and not awake?
A thought?
Nothing?
Aren't they just words?
What do you mean by awake?
I put it out there as the perfect state.
It's not a state, you say.
Is being awake for me impossible?
The me can't wake up.
I am awake.

74.

I'm close to giving up.
Is that a good thing,
or a bad thing?

75.

How can I connect with anyone,
when I'm the only one here?
I'm the only one.
I'm one as everything,
everything is one.
I am one.
I guess one can't get more connected than that.

76.

Without thought,
time can no longer exist.
The illusion of time is just made up of thought.
Does that mean nothing ever happened?
If I don't go to thought, there is only now.
A sad feeling of losing everything,
of losing everyone, hits me like a gigantic wave.
Being nothing in a big ocean of nothing.
Like I'm waking up from a dream,
it's all gone, it never did exist.
It leaves an empty feeling that lingers,
and slowly, slowly it disappears.
But it's all thought.
Nothing ever happened.

77.

I am a wizard.
Magically I see thoughts for what they are.
Thought has no meaning.
I let them be.
I no longer follow them here and there
till I'm mesmerised out of reality.

78.

I AM Awake!

79.

Everything is mostly empty space,
and so am I.
In between every thought,
there is mostly empty space.
I am empty space.
Between every emotion,
in between objects that are seen,
empty space, empty space.
Every object is mostly empty space.
Nothing is all there is,
empty beautiful nothing.
I'm everything and I'm nothing.
Empty space is what I am,
and everything in between.
In between what?
In between Nothing?

80.

I can sense a drowsy feeling
when hypnotised by the mind.
The thought-world makes sight less crispy,
hearing goes blurry and the body tenses up.
I can feel the tension when a thought gets my attention,
and drags me into the land of illusion.
But when I catch myself,
I feel a relaxation in body and mind,
like a big outbreath of the universe.
Tension is my wake-up call.

81.

The experience of being me is a thought.
I'm dissolving into nothing.

82.

Here I am, hyper-vigilant,
looking for the next thought,
sensing the body,
listening for sounds.
But who is doing all that?
Sounds coming and going,
no need for a listener to take credit.
Thoughts moving around,
did anyone choose them,
or are they just there,
no matter if I pay attention to them or not?
Who is paying attention?
Attention given to certain parts of this body,
sensing everything.
Am I attention?
Am I awareness?
Different scents moving around in the air.
Does it have to be a me who smells the scents in the air,
or are they there, as different scents, anyway?
What is my purpose here?
Can I just relax, and do nothing?
All this doing,
when doing is not needed,
doing is not relevant.
Everything is happening without a doer,
without a me trying to control the waves
on this magnificent ocean.

83.

Strange dreams visit me at night.
Is it just a different dream that presents itself,
when the day comes upon me?
Is this all a dream?
If that is so,
isn't it time to wake up?

84.

Is me a fake?
No, me can't be a fake,
me doesn't even exist.

85.

The silence of awareness.
I have a choice, where I put my attention.
I choose to put it on the quiet space within,
the silence of consciousness,
the quietness of awareness,
the silence that is always inside me.
I'm blessed with the freedom of choice,
even though it sometimes feels like a curse.
I have the freedom to choose where I put my attention,
to sense the awareness that's aware of everything,
to sense it, be it, just be.

86.

Stop clinging to thoughts.
Just STOP!

87.

A thought cannot win me over,
but it can seem to make me drowsy,
to make me not be on my guard.
It's easy to slip into oblivion,
thinking I'm a me.
I need to be alert.
No thought can win me over,
but sometimes they seem to drug me,
and I drift away into la-la land.
No thoughts are me,
it's just a mistaken identity.

88.

Take away I, take away me.
What's left?
Feeling, seeing, hearing, smelling, tasting,
sensing, awaring.
Being empty of everything,
and full at the same time.

89.

Thoughts are moving around in space.
They do not belong to a me,
just as the sound of a raven in the sky
does not belong to a me.
It's just a sound in the sky.
The scent of newly cut grass does not belong to a me,
it's just a scent appearing in empty space.
Everything is just pulsating in emptiness,
and so is this nothingness I sense is I.
Am I the empty space?
Emotions show up,
they do not belong to a me.
Thinking veils everything from the me,
or is it from I?
What is me anyway?
Thinking seems to move me away from reality.
Thoughts are moving effortlessly in space.
They have nothing to do with a me.
They have nothing to do with reality.
And neither does the me.

90.

I'm the looking, I'm the awaring.
I'm not a subject, I'm more like a verb.

91.

Thoughts are everywhere,
it's getting nearly impossible to move between them.
What if I get stuck?

92.

Me does not exist,
me is not real,
still, here I am fighting it.
See me,
hear me.
Save me from being entangled in the me.
That does not make sense.
I'm fighting to be free,
fighting for reality,
fighting to be free to be,
free to be what I am.
I am free.
Freedom is already here,
freedom is what I am.
Still, being in bondage is how I identify myself.
My self,
there is no me, there is no my,
there is no self.
Still, it all feels so real.
It is real,
but not real.
See me.
Me is seen,
sounds appear to no-one.
I'm everything,
and everything is seen.
I'm nothing appearing as everything,
seen by no-one.

93.

I'm moving around as graceful as a bird of prey.
I stumble over words,
I do not remember what happened before I blinked.
Am I new every second that passes,
or am I as old as the beginning of time?
Time is elusive, time is an illusion.
I'm moving forward, without moving.
Then and there does not exist,
how can I be moving at all?
There's only here and now,
I'm floating in space,
moving as air moving through air,
no resistance.
Am I still alive?

94.

Save me, I'm drowning,
drowning in myself,
drowning in the illusion of being a me.

95.

My world is just a thought,
reality is not.

96.

You say I have free will.
I must will myself to not be awake,
or is it just a mistake of positioning myself
where I do not belong?

97.

What is hiding behind the I,
which can hear or sense the I?
I is just a word.
I feel it's something more.
Awareness without the word awareness.
A thought appears, trying to help,
or is it just to lead me away from what I am.
Words can't help me here,
thoughts can't help me here.
Fool me not,
I'm here to wake up,
wake up from this world
that has been created in thought.
I don't mind this world,
as long as I don't have to live in it.
It's time to wake up.

98.

I'm drowning in a sea of thoughts.
And become reborn in the ocean of consciousness.

99.

Go deep into the now, NOW,
only now.

100.

What am I?
Is I located somewhere,
or is I located everywhere?
It feels like I is somewhere.
But where?
Or am I nothing?
How to find nothing?

101.

I feel trapped,
like a bird in a cage.
And the cage gets smaller and smaller.
I'm stuck,
I can't move.
How to not try to escape?
Escape into doing,
do, do, do.
I need to surrender to life.

102.

Nothing resonates with me.
Nothing is all there is.
What about me?
the me cries out in agony.
Am I nothing?
Everything is nothing,
nothing is all there is,
nothing can never change.
Change into what,
when nothing is all there is?
I'm nothing,
no need to change,
just be.

103.

Your behaviour managed to trigger me.
Can I still wake up?
A feeling of being used,
being taken advantage of,
surfaces and takes all my attention,
it makes me so angry that I'm exploding inside.
My energy is going all over the place,
I can't focus,
I just want to crawl out of my skin.
I'm ready to disintegrate into nothing,
just to avoid this feeling.
Is this what could actually
push me to wake up?

104.

My mind contains all the memories from this life,
and more, and they all want to come up
at the same time.

105.

Will I be lonely without the voice in my head?

106.

Thought is rewriting history.
It's simply commentating,
interpreting and distorting reality.

107.

What can I do,
when the planet is going to pieces?
What can I do?
What can I do,
when the world is going crazy?
What can I do?
How can I prevent going to pieces,
how can I avoid going crazy?
I'm grabbing for some sanity in an insane world,
to not add more insanity,
to stay in the light.
WAKE UP!
It's time to wake up!

108.

Am I trapped in a thought?
Or are thoughts trapped in me,
as an endless loop of nonsensical words and images?

109.

The rain wraps its drops around me,
soaks me from top to bottom.
I can feel all sorrows leaving my being.
Being totally naked of pain and worries,
I can enter life as I with a human body.
I feel light as a feather,
happy as a bird,
flying around,
free from the mind's concerns about
the future and the past.
Past this,
there is no going back.
Past this,
there's only,
this.

110.

I realised that I am a thought,
but I didn't realise that the I that realised that
I am a thought is also a thought.

111.

I'm the dance of nothingness.
As I walk like a shadow in the night,
I leave no trace in my wake.
I am awake.

Love is the answer